Washington! Adventures for Kids

An Activity Guide for Children

by
Marti Weston and Florri DeCell

Illustrated by Elizabeth Wolf

Published by
Vandamere Press
a division of AB Associates
P. O. Box 5243
Arlington, VA
22205

Second Edition

Second Printing, August 1993

ISBN 0-918339-13-8

Library of Congress Catalog Number
90-070168

First Edition Published 1983 by Children's Innovations

Manufactured in the United States of America. This book is set in
ITC Bookman Light.

ACKNOWLEDGMENTS

We are indeed happy to be able to present this new and expanded edition of **Washington! Adventures for Kids**. In rewriting this book we have missed the enthusiasm and insights of our former partner, Heidi Simmons, who moved to Connecticut shortly after our first printing. We thank her for her long-distance encouragement.

As with our first edition, Carol Hurwitz and Gladys Stern at Georgetown Day School have been extremely helpful. We deeply appreciate the willingness of the information officers and museum guides at each site to answer our many questions and to share so generously their time and knowledge. We especially thank Maria Spencer at the Parks and History Association for encouraging our venture from the beginning.

Our special thanks and appreciation to our husbands for their unwavering support and our children for their incredible patience. And we especially thank Elmo and Ella Pascale for joining us on trips to the museums so our children could have extra snack breaks.

Hours and Addresses

In order sites appear in this book

Capitol Hill

United States Capitol
9:00 am-4:30 pm daily
(202)224-3121/(202)225-6827 (tours)

Supreme Court
1st and East Capitol Street, NE
9:00 am-4:30 pm, weekdays
tours: 9:00 am-3:30 pm, weekdays, when court is not in sesseon.
(202)479-3000

Library of Congress
10 1st Street, SE
8:30 am-9:30 pm, Monday-Friday;
8:30 am-6:00 pm, Saturday;
1:00 pm-5:00pm, Sunday
(202)707-5000

The Smithsonian

National Air and Space Museum
6th Street and Independence Avenue, SW
10:00 am-5:30 pm daily except Christmas
(202)357-2700

Hirshhorn Museum and Sculpture Garden
8th Street and Independence Avenue, SW
10:00 am-5:30 pm daily except Christmas
(202)357-2700

National Gallery of Art
West Building
6th Street and Constitution Avenue, NW
East Building
4th Street and Constitution Avenue, NW
10:00 am-5:00 pm, Monday-Saturday
9:00 pm April 1-Labor Day;
noon-9:00 pm, Sundays
(202)737-4215

National Museum of Natural History
10th Street and Constitution Avenue, NW
10:00 am-5:30 pm daily except Christmas
(202)357-2700

National Museum of American History
Between 12th and 14th Streets and Constitution Avenue, NW
10:00 am-5:30 pm daily except Christmas
(202)357-2700

Monuments and Memorials

The Washington Monument
15th Street, NW, on the Mall
9:00 am-5:00 pm daily, September-March;
9:00 am-midnight, April-August.
Closed Christmas.
(202)426-6839

The Lincoln Memorial
23rd Street, NW, in West Potomac Park
Open 24 hours daily
(202)426-6895

The Jefferson Memorial
Tidal Basin
8:00 am-midnight daily except Christmas
(202)426-6821

The Kennedy Center
New Hampshire Avenue, NW and
Rock Creek Parkway
Tours: 10:00 am-1:00 pm, daily
(202)254-3600

Historic Sites

Arlington National Cemetery
and Arlington House
Arlington, Virginia
8:00 am-5:00 pm daily, October-March;
8:00 am-7:00 pm daily, April-September
545-6700 (Arlington Cemetery)
557-0613 (Arlington House)

Mount Vernon
Mount Vernon, Virginia
9:00 am-5:00 pm daily, March-October
9:00 am-4:00 pm daily, November-February
(703)780-2000

Most of these sites have extended summer hours that vary depending on annual budgets. Please check with each location for hours and tour details.

Table of Contents

Can you identify these buildings?

1. ______________________________

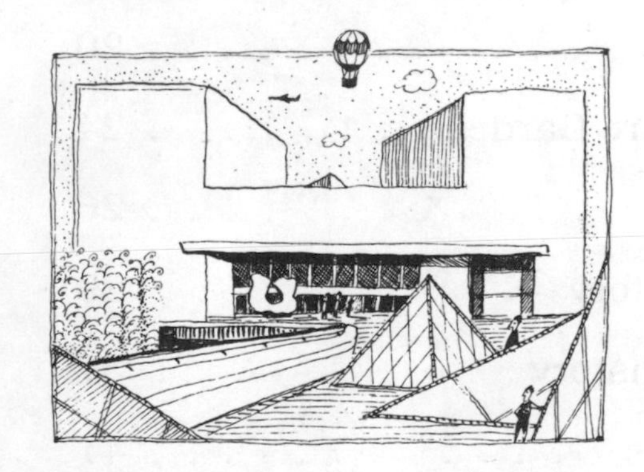

2. ______________________________

3. ______________________________

4. ______________________________

5. ______________________________

6. ______________________________

Introduction

Over the years we have taken children on dozens of field trips to the wonderful sights of Washington, D.C. But there is so much to see—so many museums to visit, so much history and science and nature to discover. To combat the glazed eyes and listless shuffles that can come from trekking through room after room of artifacts, we began making activity sheets that helped focus the children's attention and gave them a sense of purpose as they looked at the exhibits.

Washington! Adventures for Kids evolved from these activity sheets. Making a game of finding things and actively engaging yourself in looking carefully makes it possible for you not only to enjoy your visits but also to learn more and to remember what you see. We hope that this book will help you look more carefully, learn more thoroughly, and, most of all, better enjoy the fourteen exciting places it covers in our nation's capital.

The book tells you a little about the history or purpose of each place you visit; then it's on to the activities. To complete them, all you need is a pencil—and an appetite for fun. It helps to read over each activity before you begin. And working with a brother or sister or friend or parent is sometimes even more fun.

A few suggestions for successful trips: Stop at the information desk at each site for a free map or information. Plan visits that last only a few hours at most; the activities for each site in this book generally take less than an hour. And before you start something else, take a break. When visiting a large museum, choose one or two exhibits to look at closely; this makes the visit more interesting than wandering aimlessly through vast halls.

Most of all, have a wonderful time. Keep this book as a memento. We have left a blank page for you to add pictures, postcards, or other remembrances of your Washington adventures.

Chapter One

Capitol Hill

The Nation's Centerpiece

George Washington was not only the first President of the United States of America, he also picked the site for the nation's new Capital city. In 1790 the Congress, which had been meeting in New York, approved Washington's choice of land along the Potomac River not far from his home in Virginia and more or less centrally located in the new nation.

The next year Pierre L' Enfant, a Frenchman, was hired to design the city. What is now the District of Columbia—called Washington, D.C., in honor of "the father of our country"—was in 1791 farmland and wilderness between the ports of Georgetown and Alexandria. L' Enfant's job as architect of the city was to plan everything from where the streets would go to where the important buildings of the new government would be located. In the midst of the open land, rising 88 feet above the Potomac River, was Jenkins Hill, which L' Enfant saw as "a pedestal waiting for a monument." This was the spot he chose for the U.S. Capitol.

Today, Jenkins Hill is called Capitol Hill, and it is here that Congress goes about its work making the laws that govern us. Here also is the Supreme Court, across the street from the Capitol and next door to the Library of Congress.

Our adventures begin with these three important sites.

The United States Capitol

Where Our Laws Are Made

Getting Started . . .

The U.S. Capitol is where the legislative branch of our government makes the laws that govern the nation. The Founders of our country decided that the national legislature would be made up of two parts, the Senate and the House of Representatives. Every state, no matter how big or small, has two Senators. The number of Representatives, however, is based on the population of the state. Wyoming, for instance, has one Representative, while California has almost 50.

New laws go through a long process before they become official. First, a Representative or a Senator writes up an idea for a new law in a special form called a bill. Once a bill is introduced in either house of Congress, it is considered by one or more committees and then talked about, or debated, before all the members. During this time, Congressmen like to hear the opinions of voters from their home states. Finally, the Members of Congress vote for or against the bill. The House of Representatives and the Senate both must vote to approve the bill. Then the

President must sign the bill for it to become a law.

You can visit the offices of your Representative or Senators in their buildings on each side of the Capitol (Senate offices are on the north and House offices on the south). Ask for special passes that allow you to sit in the visitors' galleries and watch the debates or voting procedures. (There are separate passes for the House and Senate, but you can usually get both at one office.) Ride the little subway train back to the Capitol, which is how Senators and Representatives get from their offices to the Capitol quickly. If there is a vote while you are near the subway, you will see lots of legislators hurrying toward the Capitol.

Can you name your Senators and Representative? Any Capitol policeman can tell you the Senator from your state. You must know your district to get the name of your Representative; lists of the Members of Congress are posted by all the elevators.

Senators:______________________ ______________________

Representative:______________________________

To see most of the Capitol you should take one of the official tours that leave the Great Rotunda every 15 to 20 minutes. These tours are very informative and often are peppered with interesting tidbits about the men and women who have made Congressional history. There are more than 800 works of art in the U.S. Capitol, including sculptures, mosaics, and paintings. They tell the stories of the people and the history of the United States. As you walk through the building, notice the beautiful tile floors and grand staircases.

Art History

The decorative band that encircles the Capitol dome above the Rotunda was designed by an Italian artist named Constantino Brumidi. He painted about one-third of it before he died in 1880. His work was continued by a fellow Italian, Filippo Costaggini, who completed Brumidi's painting in1888. A gap of 31 feet, 2 inches remained, probably because of a miscalculation on Brumidi's part. It wasn't until the 1950s that American artist Allyn Cox was commissioned by Congress to complete the frieze, as the painted band is called. The frieze is 58 feet above the floor, stretches around the dome for 300 feet, and is just over 8 feet tall.

Frieze Tag

Can you find the scenes on the frieze that are listed below?

Landing of Columbus, 1492
Midnight Burial of De Soto in the Mississippi, 1542
Pocahontas Saving the Life of Captain John Smith, 1607
Landing of the Pilgrims at Plymouth, 1620
Reading of the Declaration of Independence, 1776
Death of Tecumseh at the Battle of Thames (Ohio), 1813
Entry of General Scott into the City of Mexico, 1847
Discovery of Gold in California, 1848
Birth of Aviation in the United States, 1903

Capitol Art

In the Rotunda are eight large paintings about the early history of our country. Name the artist and date of each painting.

1. *Landing of Columbus at the Island of Guanahani, West Indies* Artist________________ Date______

2. *Discovery of the Mississippi by De Soto* Artist________________ Date______

3 *Baptism of Pocahontas* Artist________________ Date______

4. *Embarkation of the Pilgrims at Delft Haven, Holland* Artist________________ Date______

5. *Declaration of Independence in Congress at Independence Hall in Philadelphia* Artist________________ Date______

6. *Surrender of General Burgoyne at Saratoga, New York* Artist________________ Date______

7. *Surrender of Lord Cornwallis at Yorktown, Virginia* Artist________________ Date______

8. *General George Washington Resigning His Commission to Congress as Commander-in-Chief of the Army* Artist________________ Date______

Capitol Search

Look at the drawings below. Search for each item during your tour. We have noted the area where each can be found. Can you find the object?

1. ______________________________

Outside East Front

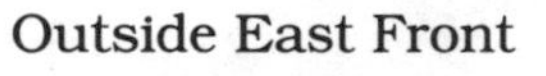

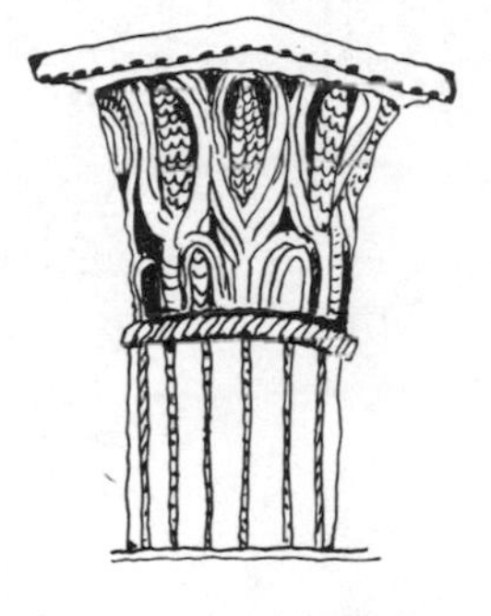

2. ______________________________

Lower East Front Entry

3. ______________________________

Lobby of Small Rotunda

4. ______________________________

Statuary Hall

5. ______________________________

In the Crypt

Capitol Trivia:

Pocahontas appears three times in the Rotunda. Can you find her?

The Supreme Court

The Highest Court in the Land

Getting Started . . .

Written more than 200 years ago, the U.S. Constitution remains the foundation of our government. To make sure that freedom and liberty would be protected, the Founding Fathers created the Supreme Court to interpret the Constitution. It is the job of the nine Supreme Court Justices, a Chief Justice and eight Associate Justices, to make sure that the legislative and executive branches of government make rules and decisions that are proper under the Constitution.

The Supreme Court mainly considers cases that are brought to it on appeal from a lower court. The Justices decide if the lower courts have followed the rules set by the government and the Constitution in settling disputes. They are helped by clerks, recent law school graduates who assist them with legal research and history. After considering a case carefully, the Justices vote. The side that gets most of the votes (the majority) wins, and an opinion is issued. Sometimes the Justices who did not agree with the majority issue a dissenting opinion.

The beautiful Supreme Court building was constructed of white

marble in 1932. Until then, the Supreme Court met in a room in the Capitol.

Supreme Court Trivia

Find these answers. Some answers you will learn when you tour the court, but some you may have to seek elsewhere.

1. Which Chief Justice was a former President of the United States?

   ____

2. Who was the first woman Justice on the Court?______________

3. What Justice played professional football?______________

4. Which Justice hiked 200 miles on the Chesapeake and Ohio Canal to call attention to the need for the preservation of the environment?

   ____

5. What Justice was called the "Great Dissenter"?______________

6. What early Chief Justice quit the Court to run for governor of New York?

   ____

Judicial Maze

Followed correctly, the maze spells out the Supreme Court's motto that is carved on the front of the building.

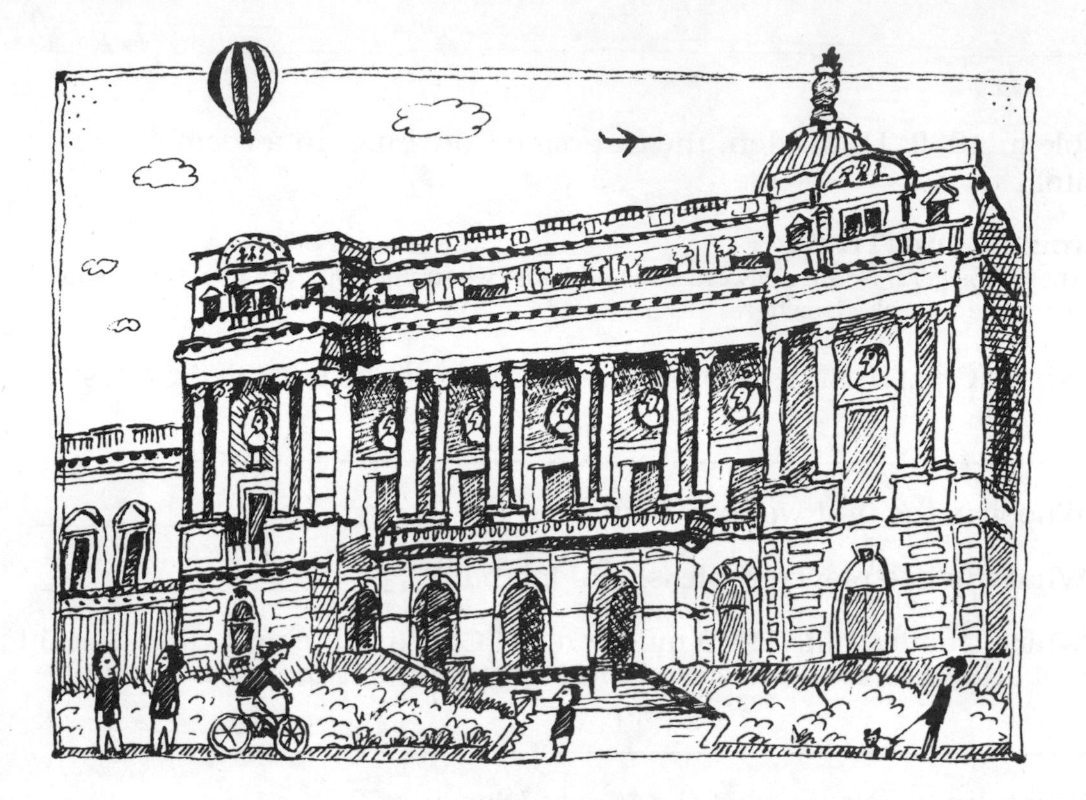

THE LIBRARY OF CONGRESS

THE BIGGEST LIBRARY IN THE WORLD

Getting Started . . .

In 1800 Congress spent $5000 to buy books for a library, which was located in thc Capitol. When the British invaded Washington in August 1814 during the War of 1812, however, the Capitol was burned, and the small library with it. Thomas Jefferson offered his personal book collection—thought to be the best in the United States at that time—as a replacement, and these books became the first permanent collection. The Library moved out of the Capitol and into the Thomas Jefferson building in 1897.

The Library of Congress lends books only to Members of Congress and their staffs, but other adults may use the Library's resources. The Library's Congressional Research Service assists the Congressional offices when a Congressman or Senator needs information on a particular topic.

The Library of Congress is the biggest library in the world. Placed in one row, the bookshelves would stretch for 535 miles, roughly the

distance from Washington to Cincinnati, Ohio. About 5000 people work in the three huge buildings that make up the Library of Congress today: the Thomas Jefferson Building (the original building), the John Adams Building, and the James Madison Building. These buildings together house more than 26 million books and pamphlets in 470 languages. In addition to books, there are music scores, magazines, films, photos, papers, maps, and many other things. Nearly 7000 items are added to the Library daily.

Be sure to see the Gutenburg Bible, one of the first printed Bibles, on display in the Great Hall of the Thomas Jefferson Building. You can also make an appointment to see the collection of violins, including several made by Antonio Stradivari, and other musical instruments in the Music Division. The copyright exhibit in the Madison Building displays prototypes, or samples, of some of the interesting items that have been copy-protected, including the first Barbie doll.

Library of Congress Word Hunt

In the scrambled letters, circle the words listed below. Answers may be vertical, horizontal, or on the diagonal.

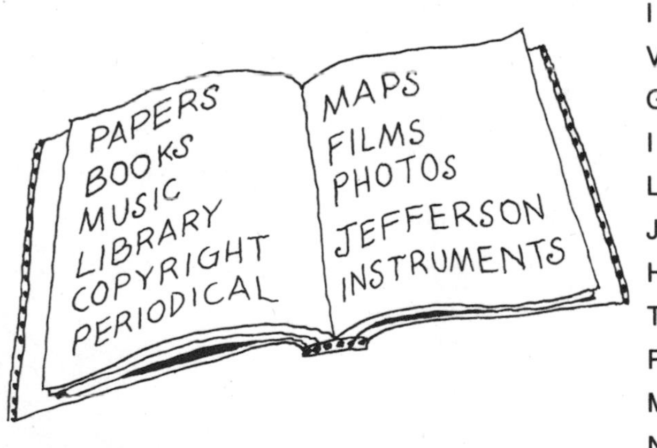

K N L N B X M M A H M E N R P U
I G P E R I O D I C A L A N A R
V Z E Q P H O T O S E O G W P M
G Z N A I O D Z N V F U V W E D
I C E E L O L X S A W I D I R D
L N N B G M U S I C C G L T S T
J J S Q G L B R T B X A E M N X
H R V T M S H R S V Q L I H S J
T V M W R J E F F E R S O N Y I
R B L Q E U J E H Q O C G S O R
M O I C Z C M V M A P S K V X I
N O B I I X H E A O X I T Q S F
V K R Q Q Q H N N T Y B B Q W H
W S A X R W S N Q T R K I Z M F
E C R W R V H B U E S M N Z M J
A A Y C O P Y R I G H T L E Q Y
A J R U A X N Z D W O F M N R O

Chapter Two

The Smithsonian Institution

Inside the Nation's Attic

The Smithsonian is a huge institution made up of many museums and research facilities, on and off the Mall. Behind the scenes of each museum are scientists, anthropologists, historians, and others who do research in their special fields.

This great institution was started not by an American but by an Englishman, James Smithson, who gave "...the whole of my property . . . to the United States of America to found at Washington, under the name of the Smithsonian Institution, an Establishment for the increase and diffusion of knowledge . . . ." This marvelous gift has grown into a vast collection of art and artifacts. The collection is so huge that you only see a tiny part of it—about 1 percent—when you visit the museums.

How does the Smithsonian get all these things? Just about everything has been donated over the years. In fact, the Smithsonian is sometimes called the "Nation's Attic" because it is filled with things that were too important to throw away but no one really knew what else to do with them. Through the years, the curators have made many valuable and important additions to the collections. Today the Smithsonian offers terrific opportunities for learning and fun.

On the following pages we explore some of our favorite exhibits in several of the Smithsonian's museums.

National Air and Space Museum

Up, Up, and Away!

Getting Started . . .

The National Air and Space Museum is a wonderland of flying machines, from simple balloons to complex rocket engines. You can see them by walking around on your own or by taking one of the tours that leave frequently from the tour desk.

In 1782, two Frenchmen, Joseph and Etienne Montgolfier, invented the hot air balloon. Because of the danger thought to be involved in flying the balloon, they could not convince King Louis XVI to allow a manned balloon flight. So the passengers on the first flight were a sheep, a rooster, and a pig. The animals went up on November 21, 1783, and came down safely, except for a slight injury to the rooster's leg. Ballooning became a popular pastime.

During this time Benjamin Franklin was in Paris serving as the United States' first Ambassador to France. From his balcony he could see the various sites where balloons took off in flight. When he returned to America, he was one of the most enthusiastic fans of ballooning.

Flying vehicles have changed a lot since the time of the Montgolfi-

ers' invention. As you explore the National Air and Space Museum, notice how each vehicle was used. Did it explore space, fight in a war, or take part in an endurance race? Is it a model, a life-size replica, or the real thing?

We take airplane travel for granted today, but it was only at the beginning of this century that Orville and Wilbur Wright first flew a power-driven airplane successfully. Orville Wright was airborne for 12 seconds at Kitty Hawk, North Carolina, in 1903. Just 66 years later, in 1969, the United States put a man on the moon.

Before leaving the Air and Space Museum, you might enjoy trying the freeze-dried ice cream used by astronauts in space.

Interesting Names

What did these vehicles of flight do?

Starfighter (between Milestones of Flight and Air Transportation)

____

Voyager (In the Main Entrance near the Independence Avenue doors)

____

GOES (Gallery 100)

____

Winnie Mae (Gallery 109)

____

Grumman Goose (Air Transportation)

____

Glamorous Glynnis (Milestones of Flight)

____

Vin Fiz (Gallery 208)

____

Rocket Word Hunt

Check each item below when you see it in the National Air and Space Museum. After your visit, circle the words in the Rocket Word Hunt. Answers are vertical, horizontal, and on the diagonal.

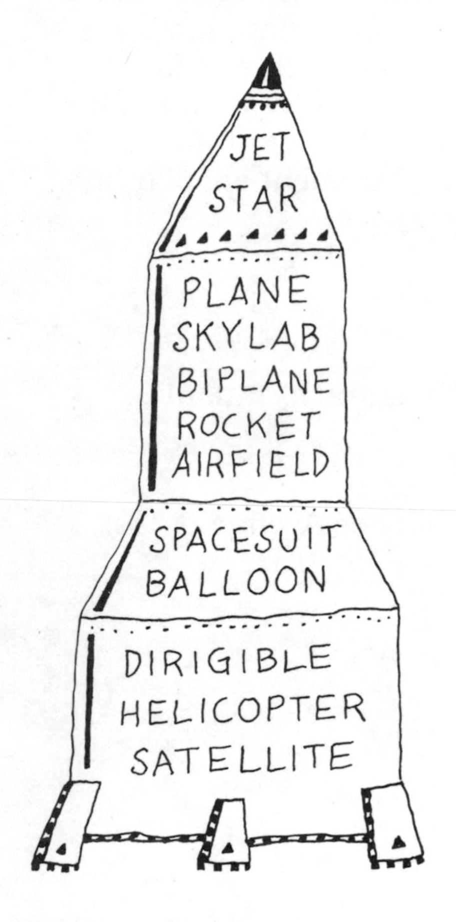

N Z U P L A N E T N M D
T W H O J D G G L Y S Z
X T P E X I Z M O Q A P
A N Y O L R K X G A T H
O J E T A I X B R Y E O
T I Q A Y G C U L X L A
Z A D M K I Q O M Q L N
S K Y L A B X A P M I T
N H G L A L B Z W T T X
Y Z S B G E N N X H E A
A Q T L Y T O L I N O R
I X A T D O S N B J X B
R Y R W L K R A I Q R L
F O H L Z G K O Y K T M
I Z A Y M U X T C Q W C
E B I P L A N E B K Y G
L W X H A K M Y J Q E F
D N N S P A C E S U I T

Flight Trivia:

What do these women have in common?____________________________

Alys McKey Bryant
Ruth Law
Harriett Quimby
Blanche Stuart Scott
Helene Dutrieu
Matilde Moisant
Bessica Raiche
Marjorie and Katherine Stinson

Fabulous Flying Feats

See directions below.

Amelia Earhart

Neil A. Armstrong

Engene Bullard and Bessie Coleman

Charles Lindberg

Wilbur and OrvilleWright

Jacqueline Cochran

First black Americans to become licensed pilots.

Flew the first power-driven airplane at Kitty Hawk in 1903.

First woman to fly faster than the speed of sound.

First man to walk on the moon on July 20, 1969. What did he say about his first step?

First woman to make a solo airplane flight across the Atlantic Ocean.

Flew the first non-stop solo flight across the Atlantic.

Match the famous flyers with their accomplishments. Look for the answers in and above Gallery 100 (Milestones of Flight) and in Gallery 208 (Pioneers of Flight).

Hirshhorn Museum and Sculpture Garden

Modern Art at a Glance

Getting Started . . .

The Hirshhorn Museum and Sculpture Garden houses the art collection of Joseph Hirshhorn, who gave it to the people of the United States as an expression of thanks for the great opportunity the country gave him, a poor immigrant boy from Latvia.

Joseph Hirshhorn's interest in art began when, as a boy, he discovered reproductions of paintings in an insurance company calendar. He cut them out and pasted them on his bedroom wall. Later, Mr. Hirshhorn displayed his real paintings and sculptures in his house and gardens in Greenwich, Connecticut. Now his collection and the museum's more recent acquisitions are beautifully displayed for all to see on the Mall. Be sure to see the Sculpture Garden; it's one of our favorite places to take a break as well as to enjoy the sculpture.

The Hirshhorn collection emphasizes Modern art (late 1800s to the present). Some artists try to make their work look realistic—or, like real life. Others do not—their paintings and sculptures, like many of those in the Hirshhorn collection, are said to be abstract. Which do you prefer?

Material Questions

Some abstract sculptures move and are called mobiles. Those that do not move are called stabiles. Can you find sculptures made with the following materials?

Material	Name of Sculpture	Artist
Alabaster	________________	____________
Aluminum	________________	____________
Bronze	________________	____________
Iron	________________	____________
Marble	________________	____________
Terra Cotta	________________	____________

How many Calder mobiles can you find?

Three Sculptures

We found three very different sculptures. See if you can find them and note the artist and date of the work.

1. Can you find a sculpture that tells the story of a Greek Myth? (2nd floor)

____

2. Can you find a sculpture that looks as though the artist might have collected smooth colorful pieces of glass at the beach? (3rd floor lounge. Careful! Don't walk on the rug—it's art!)

____

3. Can you find a sculpture that looks as though the artist might have found pieces at a junkyard? (3rd floor)

____

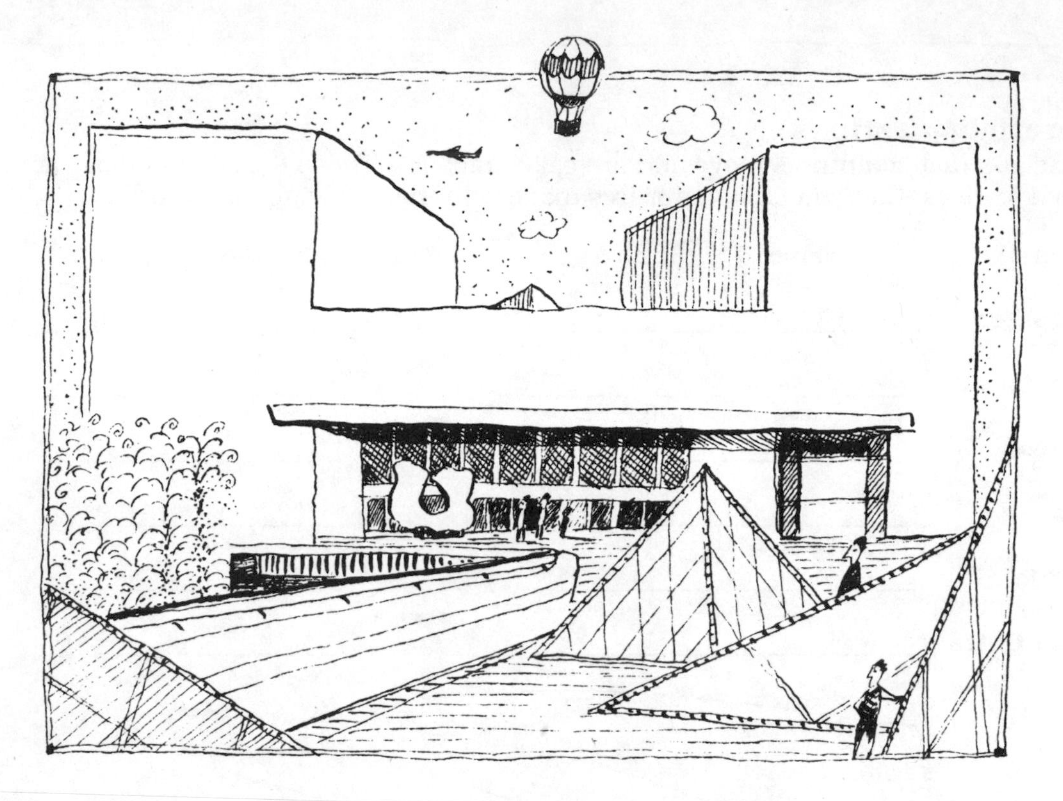

National Gallery of Art

Great Art of the Western World

Getting Started . . .

The National Gallery of Art is one of the finest art museums in the world. In 1937, Andrew Mellon gave the United States Government his magnificent art collection. He also provided $15 million for the construction of the museum.

Two buildings make up the National Gallery. The older, original building is called the West Building. Across 4th Street is the East Building (illustrated above), designed by I.M. Pei and completed in 1978. Today, the two buildings house art and artifacts dating from the 13th century to the present, including artwork from the original Mellon gift as well as donations from many other people.

While you're exploring the gallery, be on the lookout for an artist painting at an easel. Often you'll see someone at work copying a gallery painting. It's a marvelous way to see how a painting is done.

If you need a break, try our favorite resting spot, the ground floor of the East building where you can look up at a huge Calder mobile. While in the West Building, sit for a few moments in the quiet Garden Courts.

Gallery Search

Can you find?	Painting	Artist
A portrait of a child	________	________
A portrait of an animal	________	________
A picture of a group	________	________
A seascape	________	________
A cityscape	________	________
A big flower	________	________
A still life	________	________

Name Game:

Fit the names of these artists in the grid below.
We did the first one to get you started.
Hint: One name appears twice.
Do you know which of these artists was a woman?________________

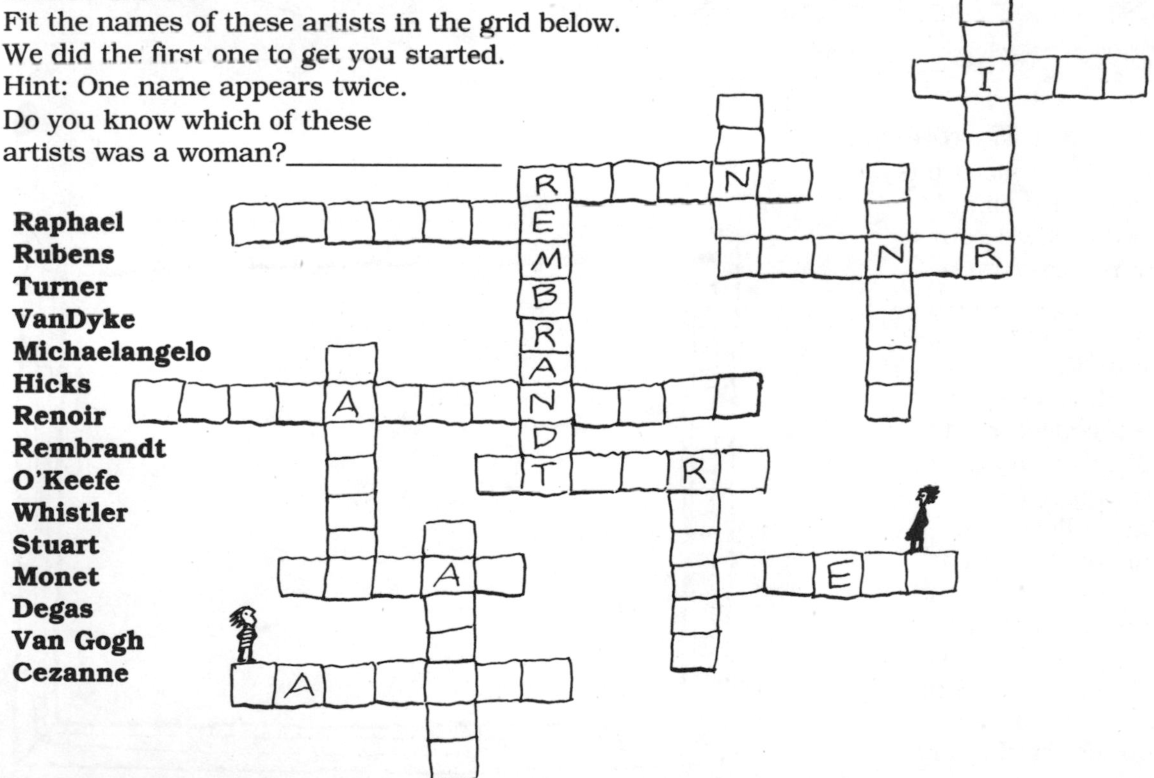

Raphael
Rubens
Turner
VanDyke
Michaelangelo
Hicks
Renoir
Rembrandt
O'Keefe
Whistler
Stuart
Monet
Degas
Van Gogh
Cezanne

Palette Puzzle

Each circle on the paint pallette contains a word puzzle. Find the starting letter, then move clockwise around the circle to discover the answer, using every letter. If you find more than one word in the circle, choose the one that has something to do with art.

In Other Words

They say a picture is worth a thousand words. Now's your chance to paint a picture with words. For this activity, go to the East Building's permanent collection of 20th Century art on the Upper Level. This collection is mostly abstract art. Take a look around and find a painting that you like for its colors or shapes or the way it makes you feel, and tell its story.

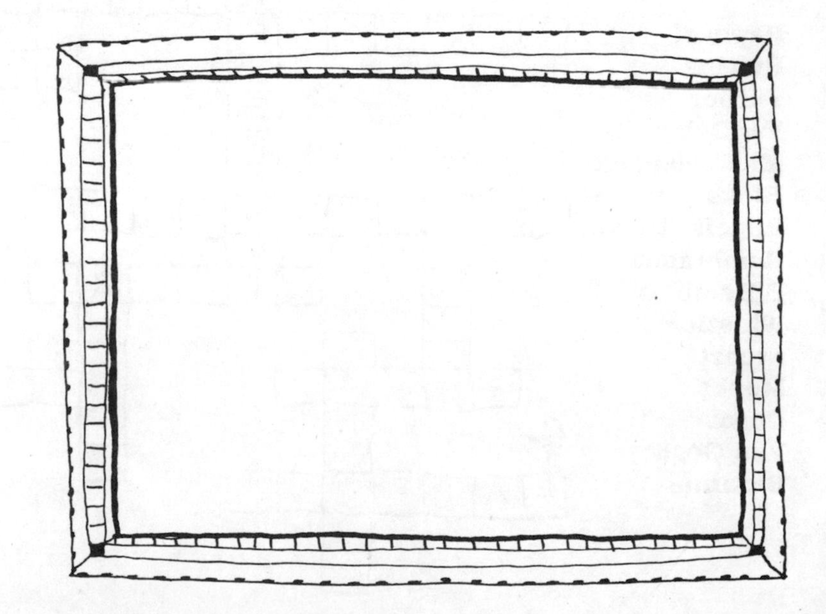

National Museum of Natural History

Where the Wonders of Nature Unfold

Getting Started . . .

In the National Museum of Natural History you can see natural science exhibits on human and animal life, the earth and environment, and outer space. More than 118 million items make up the museum's collection, but less than 1 percent (still almost a million objects) are on display at any one time.

Check out the **Dinosaur Hall**, where you can study the bones of the huge reptiles that roamed the earth millions of years ago. Note that some bones are actual fossils, while others are made of a plastic compound. Sometimes the paleontologists complete a partial fossil with plastic. A paleontologist is someone who studies prehistoric forms of life through plant and animal fossils.

The **Mineral and Gem** exhibit will make you want to become a rock collector. In this hall there are minerals and gems of every shape, color, and degree of hardness. Considered to have the best mineral collection in the world, the Smithsonian displays only 3 out of every 100 minerals it has. The gem collection, thought to be the second best after the British crown jewels, includes the biggest blue diamond in the world, the Hope diamond.

In **Life in the Sea**, you will want to look at the living coral reef, the mollusks, and Hydrolab, an underwater research vehicle.

Most of the things you see in the **Native American Hall** depict Native American life as it was when settlers were moving into what is now the United States. When you reach the totem pole, turn left and enter another hall that shows how Native Americans lived in the distant past, before explorers and settlers began arriving in the New World.

NATIVE AMERICAN HALL

Great Word Hunt

Find the following words
in the Teepee.
The words may be vertical,
horizontal,
or diagonal.

cups
toys
houses
boxes
masks
bows
baskets
tools
canoes
knives
jewelry
spears
bowls
arrows
totem poles
clothes
fishing nets
travois

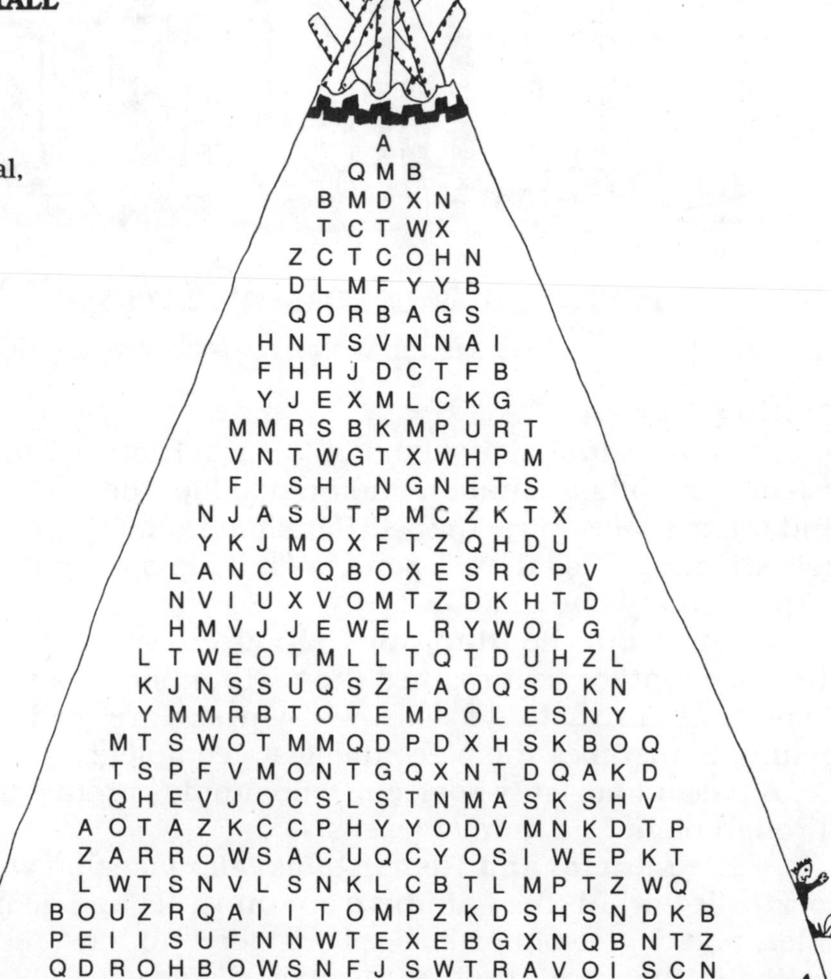

What Kind of Hunter Are You?

Native Americans had to make almost everything they used in daily life. In the exhibits, find the items listed below. Next to each item, write the material that was used to make it.

toys ____________________

houses ____________________

masks ____________________

kayaks/canoes ____________________

knives ____________________

jewelry ____________________

spears ____________________

bowls ____________________

totem pole ____________________

Homework

Places all over the United States have Native American names. For instance, the name for Maryland's Chesapeake Bay comes from an Indian word that means "Great Shellfish Bay."

Go to the library or historical society near where you live. Ask the people who work there to help you look up names in your area that come from Indian words.

THE INSECT ZOO

The Insect Zoo exhibits insects in their natural habitats. Insects are a type of arthropod. Other types, or classes, of arthropods are listed on the wall as you enter the zoo.

Notice that some of the insects are hard to spot because they blend in with their surroundings. This is called camouflage. What are some of the ways that these insects blend in?

Discover which arthropods go through distinct stages in their life cycles.

Notice also how arthropods eat. Some, like the mosquito, suck their food. Others chew, absorb, or filter the foods they eat. As you observe the arthropods' eating habits, you will see that they eat many different kinds of foods. You may even see one arthropod eating another.

Crack This Code:

Do you know where the word arthropod comes from? To find out, cross out every other letter starting with the second one. The letters remaining should be written on the blanks below the coded message.

For example:

g i r n a y s u s t h n o k p l p u e m r o = grasshopper

Now it's your turn:

A y r n t s h k r i o m p z o t d y   c s o b m b e d s c

____

f y r t o z m j   a x   L u a h t y i l n y   w k o p r f d z

____

m q e x a v n a i h n s g y   j y o l i z n s t h e z d n   l c e n g t s z

____

Insect Zoo Crossword Puzzle

Complete this crossword puzzle using the clues and looking around the Insect Zoo.

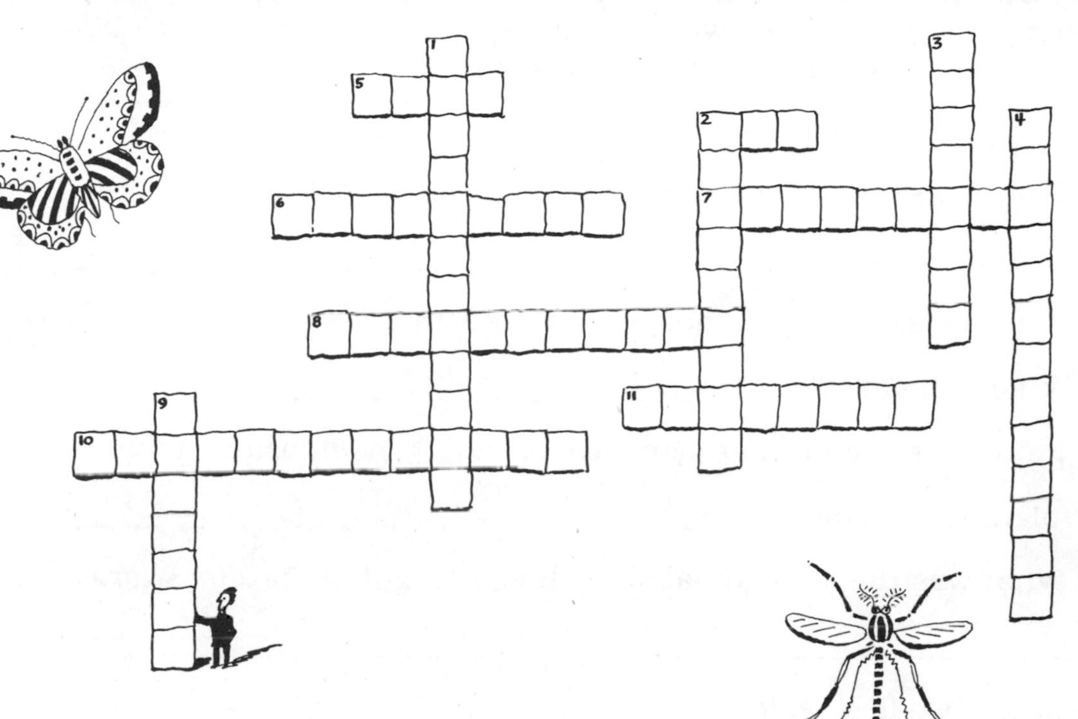

Across:

2. This flying insect lives in a highly organized society called a hive.

5. This tasty arthropod lives in the ocean, bay, or on land. It has a hard shell and claws with pincers at the end.

6. This arthropod has many body sections with two pairs of legs on each section.

7. This arthropod is a large furry spider. At the Insect Zoo you may be able to watch it being fed.

8. This arthropod jumps great distances, can eat many plants in a short time, and causes problems for gardeners.

10. This arthropod has a shell that is in two parts. Its tail is long and pointed which helps it turn over as it swims.

11. This insect makes silk thread.

Down:

1. The stick-like shape of this arthropod is a form of camouflage.

2. The life cycle of this arthropod is in four stages. In its last stage it often has colorful wings.

3. We consider this insect a pest. It gets its food by sucking the blood of other animals—including people.

4. This arthropod gets its food by chewing up other arthropods. It's green and often moves its front legs in a way that makes it look like it is praying. A larger cousin from the Amazon region in Brazil eats small animals.

9. On warm nights you can hear this arthropod make a lovely chirping sound by rubbing parts of its forewings together. Some people believe this insect brings good luck.

DINOSAUR GALLERY

The Dinosaur Gallery is one of the museum's most popular exhibits. We think you'll understand why as soon as you walk in and meet *Diplodocus*, *Tyrannosaurus rex*, and a few of their friends.

Fossil Find

1. Find the skeleton of a dinosaur that is as big as two elephants. What is it called? ______________________________
2. Find the skeleton of a horned dinosaur that probably lived in herds. What is it called? ______________________________
3. Find the skeleton that may have been a baby dinosaur. What else might it have been?______________________________
4. What was the approximate length and height of *Tyrannosaurus rex*?

   ____
5. Name two flesh eaters.______________________________
6. Name three plant eaters.______________________________
7. Find the exhibit of bones that represents a place where what may have been a *Stegosaurus* was discovered. Name some tools that a paleontologist uses. ______________________________
8. Fossils can be soft and crumbly. After they are cleaned and sprayed with a preservative, they are sometimes wrapped in______________.

Homework

Find the Jurassic Period diorama. When you get home, can you find a box and construct a similar scene?

Minerals and Gems

Gem Seeking

There are minerals and gems from all over the world. Find one from each of the following countries.

Country	Mineral or Gem Name	Color
Mexico	__________	__________
Brazil	__________	__________
Japan	__________	__________
Russia	__________	__________
Germany	__________	__________
Italy	__________	__________
Yugoslavia	__________	__________
England	__________	__________
Sweden	__________	__________

State Stones

There are also minerals and gems from the United States. Can you find a mineral or gem that was found in your home state?__________

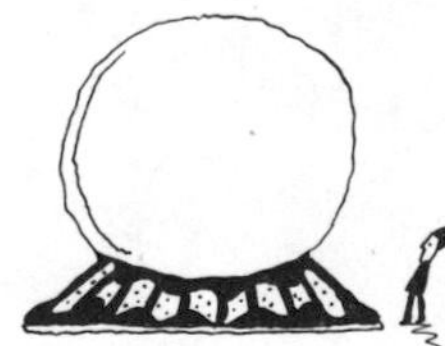

Can you find: the Hope diamond?
the crystal ball?
the giant quartz that fills a whole display window?

LIFE IN THE SEA

Mollusks can be simply defined as shelled animals, although they come in many shapes and forms. They can live in sea or fresh water, on land, or in mud, sand, or rocks. A thin tissue, called a mantle, secretes a limy substance that becomes the shell. Notice how the shells in this exhibit vary in size, shape, and texture.

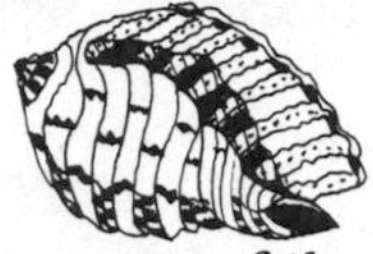

Describe That Mollusk!

Choose a shell. In the blanks write the scientific name and, if possible, the name of the ocean where the shell is found. Then circle the words that describe the shell.

1. Scientific name

Ocean where it can be found

______________________ ______________________

smooth	rough	curved	ridged	coiled	flat
spiked	white	pink	tan	brown	shiny
dull	speckled			pointed	black

Water Colors

Nature's colors range from soft to vivid. This is especially so in a coral reef. Look closely at thc museum's living coral reef. Sketch your favorite section here and color it in later.

Other things to see:

LIFE IN THE ANCIENT SEA, BIRDS OF THE WORLD, SKELETONS, MOONROCKS

The National Museum of American History

The Story of America

Getting Started . . .

This Smithsonian museum specializes in collections that tell about America. There is something here for every interest: stamps, trains, coins, fashions, musical instruments, and much more. You will want to take some time to watch the pendulum, and you won't want to miss the old Fort McHenry flag when it is displayed, usually on the half hour. Then, it's on to the collections!

There are stamps from all over the world. At this collection you can discover a lot about the history of stamps as well as the development of the United States Postal Service. Special highlights of the Smithsonian's vast coin collection are the Gold Room and the exhibit of forgeries of both coin and paper currencies. The displays on trains and musical instruments are also fun and informative. Maybe you will get an idea while you are here for a collection you would like to start at home.

The collections in this museum, which come from all areas of life in America, tell the story of our country from its beginnings.

After the Revolution: Everyday Life in America, 1780-1800

In this exhibit you will learn how people lived when our country was new. The tools, musical instruments, kitchen implements, dishes, clothes, and other things they used reveal a lot about their lives.

Artifact Search

Below are drawings of many items in **After the Revolution: Everyday Life in America, 1780-1800**. Can you find and identify them?

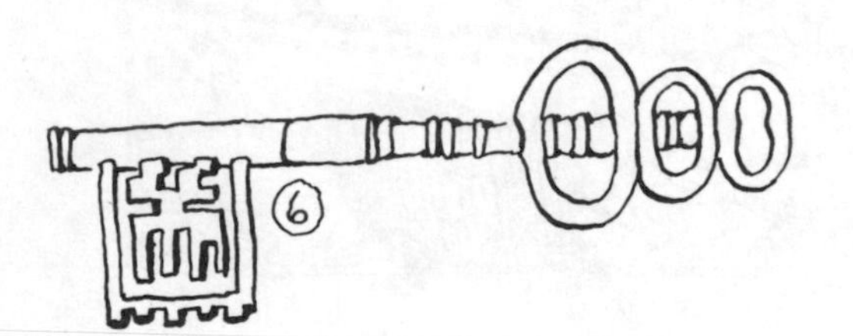

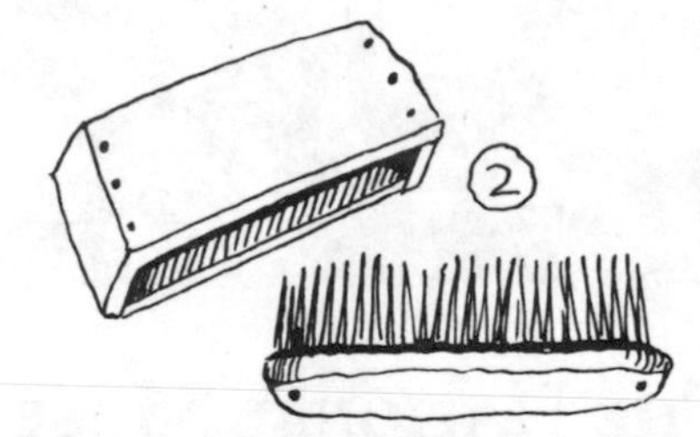

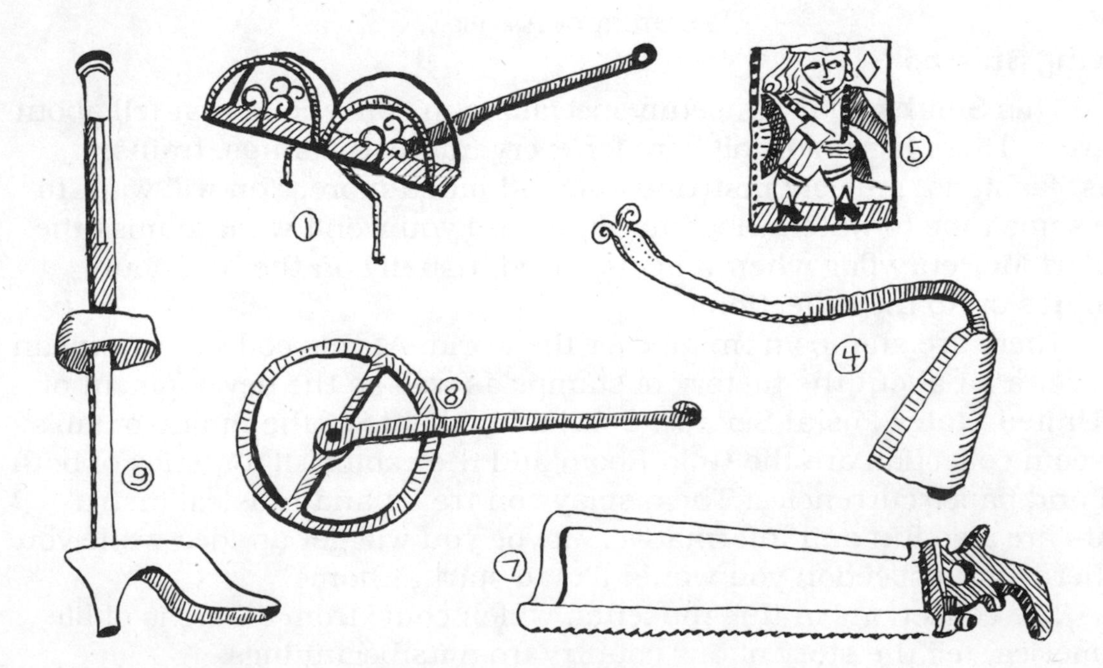

A Nation of Nations

The exhibits here tell about the many different kinds of people who came to America, bringing their own traditions and beliefs, and how, together, they built this great nation.

School Quiz

How is this schoolroom different from your classroom? List three things.

Campaign Mania

Look for the display of campaign buttons. People wear these buttons to express an opinion or to show support for a political candidate. Use this space to design a campaign button for either yourself or a real candidate.

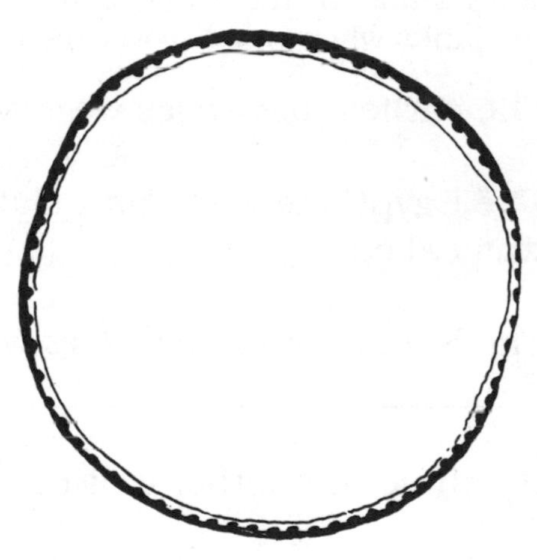

Name That Sport

Directions: In the sports exhibit there is equipment from many different sports. How many can you name?

____

____

____

THE AUTOMAT

Can you find the Horn and Hardart Automat? The automat was an unusual kind of restaurant. How did people get their food?

____

NATIONAL PHILATELIC COLLECTION

A philatelist is a stamp collector. The Smithsonian's collection, with more than 750,000 stamps on display, is one of the finest in the world. You can find out all about the postal system from the days of the Pony Express to the latest, most up-to-date machinery.

Are You a Stamp Collector?

Carefully study the history of postal services exhibit. Fill in the blanks when you discover the correct answers.

1. The earliest messages were written on ______________.
2. The Egyptians wrote on a flat, even substance that they invented. It was called ______________.
3. The Romans used couriers who rode from place to place on ______________________.
4. Parchment, another writing material, was developed in ________B.C.

Postage Trivia

Unscramble these two words to find out the name of the first Postmaster General of the United States.

n j a B i n m e   n r k i l F n a

__________________   __________________

This man believed that a good postal system should be provided by the government to allow people to exchange information easily.

Other Things To See:

FIRST LADIES' DRESSES, PRINTING PRESSES, GUNBOAT PHILADELPHIA

Chapter Three
Monuments and Memorials

Paying Tribute to the Nation's Heroes

Washington, D.C., is filled with monuments and memorials honoring people who have helped make America a great nation. Four of the city's most prominent monuments, paying tribute to four of America's best-loved presidents, are located on or near the Mall. The Washington Monument, strong and simple and straight, towers above the landscape in honor of the Father of our Country, George Washington, our greatest hero. The Jefferson Memorial honors the vision of Thomas Jefferson, who drafted our Declaration of Independence more than 200 years ago and whose ideas helped shape our government and our way of life. The Lincoln Memorial recognizes the great courage, compassion, and faith of Abraham Lincoln, who struggled to keep our nation united and to make all of our people free. The Kennedy Center is a different kind of monument—a living memorial to John F. Kennedy, whose spirit and vigor are recalled in the artistic performances given there.

When Pierre L'Enfant, the architect of Washington, laid out the city, he foresaw that it would be the Capital of a great nation. He thought it should have grand boulevards and great monuments. He would not have been disappointed in our tributes to our great leaders.

The Washington Monument

A Soaring Tribute to the Nation's Father

Getting Started . . .

The Washington Monument honors our first President, George Washington. The location was selected in 1791 by Pierre L' Enfant when Washington was still alive. The original site, however, would not support a heavy structure so the location was moved about 100 yards to the southeast. Construction of the memorial began in 1848, nearly 50 years after Washington's death, and 40 more years would pass before it was completed. The work was held up by money problems and political disagreements. In 1854, construction stopped altogether. The monument, then about 150 feet tall, sat unfinished through the Civil War. In 1880, Congress appropriated the money to finish it. The marble used to complete the Washington Monument came from a different section of the quarry so there is a line where the monument changes color slightly. Can you see it?

The Washington Monument was opened to the public on October

9, 1888. It is a little over 555 feet tall. The walls are 15 feet thick at the base and 18 inches thick at the top. The foundation goes 36 feet, 10 inches into the ground. On a perfect day you may be able to see all the way to Mount Vernon, Washington's home.

View From The Top

Look west toward the Potomac River. What do you see?________________

Look to the north. What do you see?________________________________

Look east. What do you see?_____________________________________

Look south. What do you see?___________________________________

Can you find the answers to these questions?

1. How much did it cost to build the Washington Monument?

   $______________

2. Does the monument move?_____ If so, how much?_______________

3. The original monument design by Robert Mills called for a structure at the base of the Washington Monument. Can you find out what it was?

   ____

4. How many flags fly at the Washington Monument?_________________

   What does this number represent?____________________________

Monumental Trivia:
Pierre L' Enfant and other leaders originally planned a different kind of monument. Can you find out what they had in mind?

The Lincoln Memorial

REMEMBERING THE NATION'S SAVIOR

Getting Started . . .

The Lincoln Memorial honors Abraham Lincoln, 16th President of the United States. President Lincoln is loved and remembered for keeping our nation together despite a long and bitter Civil War, and for ending slavery in the United States.

The architecture of the memorial is similar to the Parthenon, the temple to the Goddess Athena in Athens, Greece. The memorial was constructed from white Colorado-Yule marble. The inside walls are made of Indiana limestone. The pink marble on the floor is from Tennessee. The ceiling is decorated with carved laurel and oak leaves.

The statue of Lincoln, in the center chamber of the memorial, was designed by Daniel Chester French, but the Piccirilli brothers of New York did the sculpting. They used 28 blocks of Georgia white marble to make the statue.

Excerpts from two of President Lincoln's most famous speeches are inscribed on the walls on each side of the sculpture. Lincoln delivered

simple but moving speeches about the importance of freedom and equality for all people. A hundred years later, Dr. Martin Luther King, Jr., winner of a Nobel Peace prize, delivered another famous speech about freedom from the steps of the Lincoln Memorial. If you have memorized a few lines from Abraham Lincoln, you might want to learn a few lines from Dr. King's "I have a dream" speech.

Outside, at the top of the Lincoln Memorial, are two rows of state names. The lower row contains the names of the 36 states in the Union at the time of Lincoln's death. The top row contains the names of the 48 states in 1922, the year the Lincoln Memorial was dedicated.

Mural Match

Study the two murals and the two speeches in the Lincoln Memorial. Match the first lines of each speech with the description of the mural.

Speech begins . . .	Mural
1. Four score and seven years ago our fathers brought forth on this continent a new nation . . . **(Gettysburg Address)**	Shows the Angel of Truth uniting the North and South by joining their hands.
2. Fellow Countrymen: At this second appearing to take the oath of office there is less occasion for an extended address . . . **(Second Inaugural Address)**	Shows the Angel of Truth freeing a slave.

Lincoln Memorial Scramble

Read each sentence, then unscramble each word to fill in the blank.

itexnehst	1. Abraham Lincoln was the ________ President of the United States.
blamre	2. The Lincoln Memorial is made of ________.
olop	3. In front of the Lincoln Memorial is the Reflecting __________.
tesats	4. The names of __________ are inscribed around the outside at the top of the Lincoln Memorial.

Lincoln Trivia

How many answers do you already know? Discover the rest by reading a book about Lincoln. Russell Freedman's *Lincoln: A photobiography*, a Newbery Medal winner, is an exceptional book about Lincoln.

1. On what date was Abraham Lincoln born?__________________
2. He was born in what state?____________________________
3. Lincoln's parents did not know how to ________ and _________.
4. When Abraham Lincoln was seven he moved to the state of ___________. Later he moved to the state of ___________.
5. Lincoln was already __________ feet tall by the time he was sixteen.
6. In 1842 Lincoln was married to ___________________________.
7. During his Presidency the nation fought the __________________.
8. To free the slaves he signed the ___________________________.
9. Abraham Lincoln was assassinated by ________________________ while watching a play at Ford's Theatre.
10. A special funeral _____________ carried Lincoln's body on a 1,600-mile trip back to Illinois. It stopped at many towns and cities along the way so people could pay tribute to the dead President.

Monumental Trivia

The inside and outside columns at the Lincoln Monument are different. Do you know which are Ionic and which are Doric?

The Jefferson Memorial

Honoring the Architect of America

Getting Started . . .

The Jefferson Memorial stands next to the Tidal Basin, which is surrounded by Oriental flowering cherry trees. When these trees blossom in the spring, the memorial is framed with color and is one of the city's most beautiful and popular sites to visit. This memorial was dedicated in 1942 to honor Thomas Jefferson, one of the most important figures in the history of the United States.

Before he became our third President, Jefferson had already written the Declaration of Independence, helped negotiate important treaties, and served as Secretary of State for President Washington and as Vice President under President John Adams. His major duty as Vice President was to preside over the activities of the U.S. Senate. During his tenure he prepared a legislative manual to guide future presiding officers. His manual is still used today, but in the House of Representatives rather than in the Senate. During his Presidency, the United States doubled in geographic size because of the Louisiana Purchase. The next time you use an atlas, see if you can find a map that shows the Louisiana Purchase.

Jefferson was also an able architect who designed his own home, Monticello, and the University of Virginia in Charlottesville, Virginia. The Jefferson Memorial, with its dome and columns, reflects the classical style that Jefferson used in his buildings.

The great bronze statue of Jefferson is 19 feet high (5.8 meters) and weighs about 5 tons. It stands on a pedestal of black Minnesota granite. You will want to walk around the statue and look out from each side of the memorial. There is a good view of the White House from the memorial. Don't forget to read the inscriptions on each of the four panels and those around the top. They express Jefferson's beliefs on freedom, education, and progress.

If you visit the Jefferson Memorial during the day, you may want to return some evening when the entire area is brightly illuminated.

Fill in the Missing Words

Find the quotes inside the memorial; complete these statements by Thomas Jefferson:

1. . . . __________, that they are endowed by their ____________ with certain ______________ ____________, among these are ______________, ________________, and the pursuit of ____________________________.

These words are from ____________________________________.

2. . . . laws and institutions must go hand in hand with the ___________ of the ___________. As that becomes more _________, more __________, as new discoveries are made, new ____________ discovered and manners and opinions change, with the change of circumstances, institutions must advance also to ________ ________ ________ ________ _______.

3. I have __________ upon the alter of God eternal _____________ against every form of _______________ over the _______________ of man.

Jeffersonian Trivia:

As you climb the steps of the Jefferson Memorial, you can see a carving above the main entry. Who are these men?

John F. Kennedy Center for the Performing Arts

A Living Memorial to our 35th President

Getting Started...

The John F. Kennedy Center for the Performing Arts is our national cultural center as well as a living memorial to President John F. Kennedy, our 35th President. Concerts, operas, musicals, ballets, plays, and films are presented here throughout the year.

President Kennedy spoke of the value of the arts often; quotations from some of his speeches are carved into the river facade of the center. You can see them by walking out onto the River Terrace and looking up at the wall.

There are flags all over the Kennedy Center. In the Hall of States you will see flags from each of the fifty states, the District of Columbia, and the territories. In the Hall of Nations hang flags from each country officially recognized by the United States.

Throughout the center you will see many gifts given in honor of President Kennedy. These include works of art, wall coverings, chandeliers, even the marble walls and the stages themselves. The private gifts and financial support that helped build the Kennedy Center and continue to support it are from foreign countries, private organizations, and individuals. To see most of the Kennedy Center you must join one of the tours offered daily, 10:00 AM to 1:00 PM.

Kennedy Center Search

Match the illustration with the flag of the country that gave the gift. Can you find the flags in the Hall of Nations? Later you may want to color the flags.

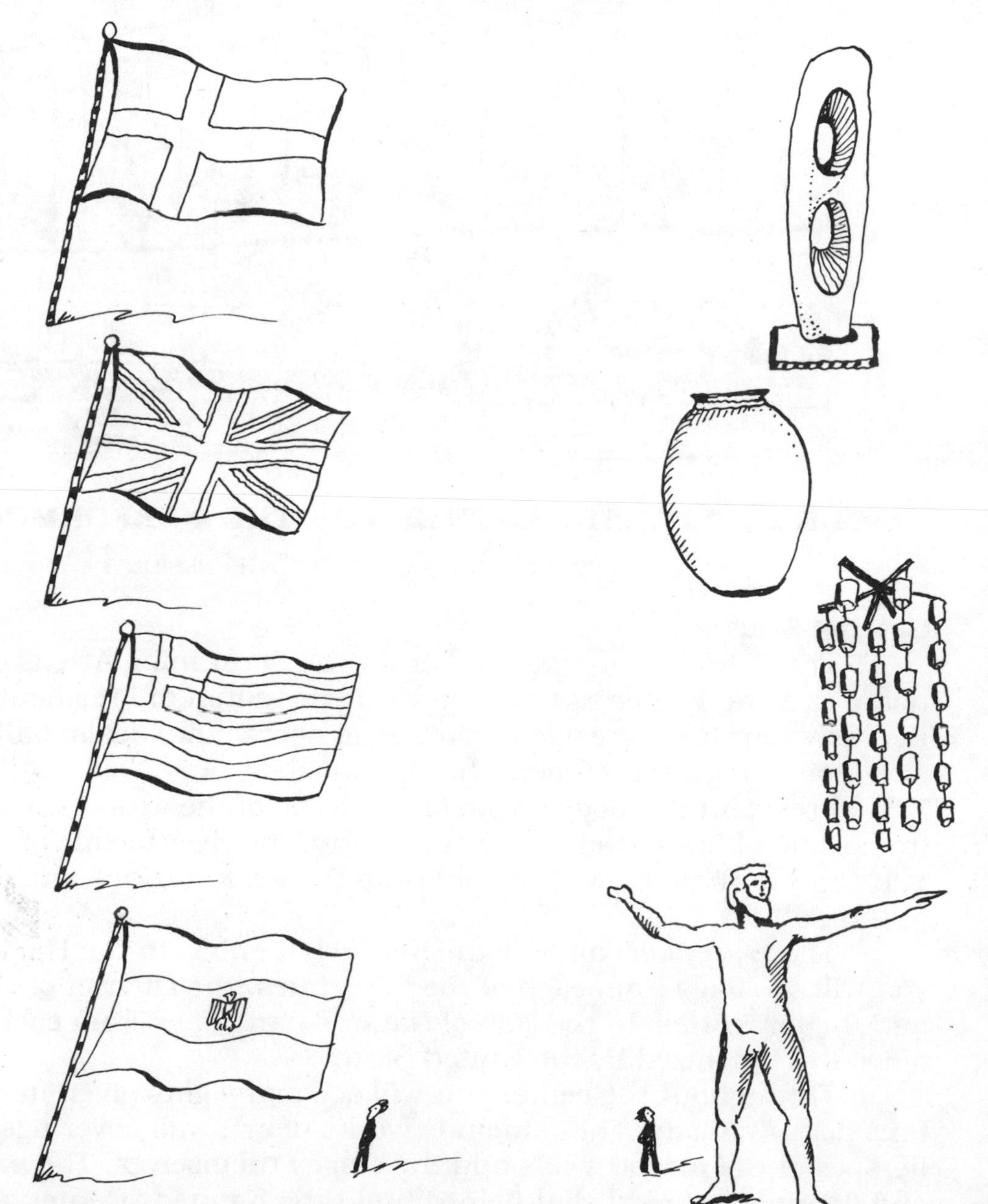

Kennedy Center Crossword Puzzle

After you take the tour you should be able to complete this crossword puzzle.

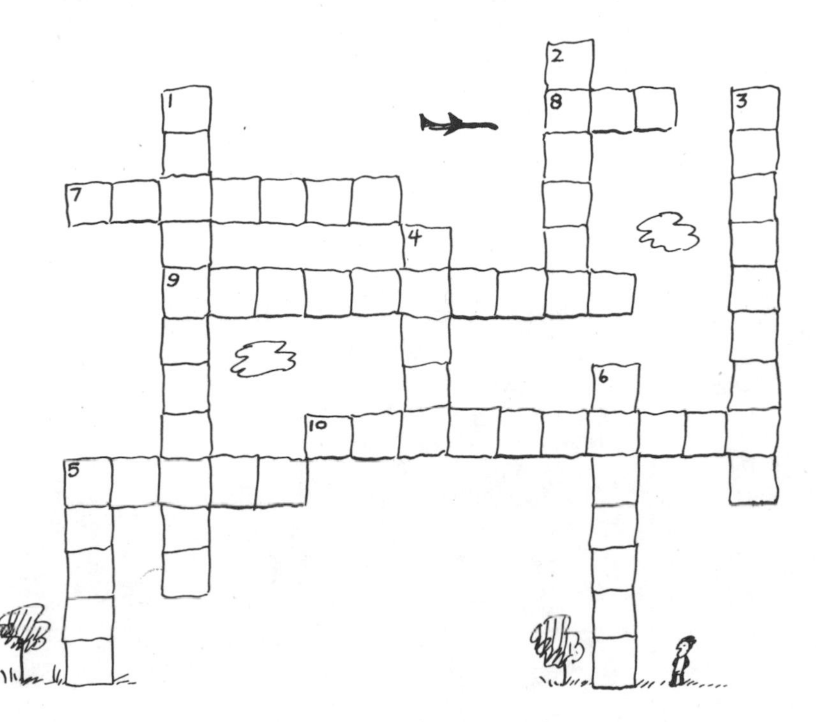

Down

1. Where orchestras, choirs, and other musicians give concerts.
2. An Italian building material used inside and out at the Kennedy Center.
3. The Kennedy Center received gifts from many of these.
4. The number of large performance halls on the first floor.
5. The grand room that is longer than two football fields.
6. The river that flows behind the Kennedy Center.

Across

5. Many of these hang in the Hall of States and the Hall of Nations.
7. The President for whom the center is named.
8. What many countries and groups gave to the Kennedy Center.
9. The theater where plays are performed that is named after the 34th President of the United States.
10. The room that has a chandelier that is 50 feet wide.

Explosive Art

Find *Apollo X 1970*, a gift from Switzerland, near the Concert Hall. How was it made?

Chapter Four

Historic Sites

Places With Important Stories to Tell

Across the Potomac River from the Capital city, in Virginia, are two fascinating places that are important parts of our nation's heritage.

Mount Vernon was the home of George and Martha Washington and their family. Seeing where and how the Washingtons lived teaches us a lot about them and about the way things were when our country was very young. The needs and ideals of the new nation were discussed in these very rooms.

Just across the river from Washington is Arlington House, the home of George Washington's adopted son, George Washington Parke Custis, and later of a great general, Robert E. Lee. Since the Civil War, Arlington House has overlooked Arlington National Cemetery, the final place of honor for thousands of men and women who have fought to preserve the same ideals George Washington fought for more than 200 years ago.

ARLINGTON NATIONAL CEMETERY AND ARLINGTON HOUSE

A FINAL TRIBUTE

Getting Started . . .

Arlington National Cemetery is the final resting place for thousands of soldiers who have served their country. It is also where many of our most respected military and government leaders are buried. Probably the most famous—and most visited—gravesites are those of President John F. Kennedy and the Tomb of the Unknown Soldier. As you follow the paths through Arlington Cemetery, you will pass the Challenger Space Shuttle Memorial, several Supreme Court Justices, and many other well-known Americans. Please be respectful here—although it is a national site for tourists to visit, it is still a cemetery and not a place to run and shout.

It is a pleasant walk to Arlington House from the Visitors Center, where an information officer will gladly mark the path for you to follow. On the way you pass the graves of President Kennedy, his brother Robert Kennedy, and the first gravesite on the property—that of a relative of the Custis-Lee family. Arlington House is situated on a bluff overlooking

Washington, D.C. Many people think this site offers the best view of the city. General Lafayette, the French officer who was a hero in the American Revolution, remarked that the view from Arlington was the best in the world.

Arlington House was built by Martha Washington's grandson, George Washington Parke Custis, who was raised at Mount Vernon by his grandparents after the death of his own father.

Custis married Molly Fitzhugh and they lived at Arlington House for the rest of their lives. Their only daughter to grow to adulthood, Mary Anna Randolph Custis, married Robert E. Lee. After their marriage, the Lees also lived at Arlington House when they were not at one of his assigned army posts.

Although Lee was a graduate of the Military Academy at West Point and served in the United States Army for over 30 years, when his home state of Virginia seceded from the Union, Lee felt obligated to accept the command of Virginia's army in 1861.

Because of the strategic location of the house, the Union army occupied it almost immediately. Mrs. Lee packed and left with her family for safer places, but many of their possessions were left behind. Most of these things, as well as the house, were lost to the Lees.

The army cut down many trees, built earthwork forts, and dug trenches around the original 1,000-acre Custis-Lee estate. In 1864, 200 acres of the Arlington House grounds were chosen to become a military cemetery for Union soldiers. On May 13, 1864, William Christman of Pennsylvania was the first soldier buried in Arlington National Cemetery.

Today, more than 200,000 Americans are buried at Arlington National Cemetery which occupies 612 acres of the Custis-Lee plantation. In 1925, Arlington House was designated a memorial to Robert E. Lee and has been restored to its 1861 graciousness.

City Vista

What do you see when you look toward Washington from the front steps of Arlington House? Write the names of important buildings you can see on the panorama below.

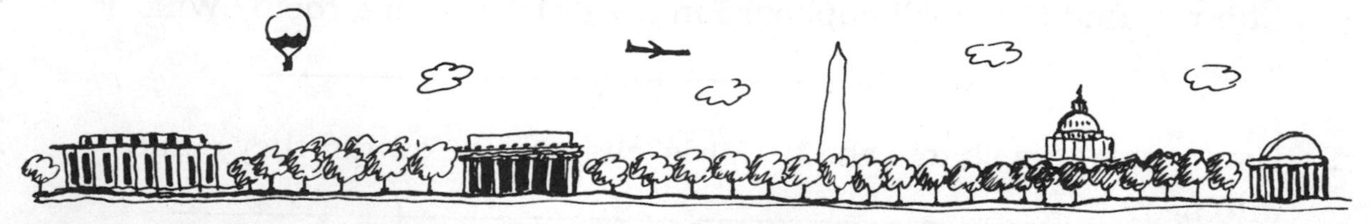

Presidential Challenge

This was a part of President Kennedy's 1961 inaugural address. The words are inscribed in the wall near his grave. Fill in the missing words.

"And so my fellow ____________: ask not what your __________ can do for you—ask what __________ can do for your country. My fellow ___________ of the ____________: ask not what ____________ will do for you, but what ______________ we can do for the __________ of man."

Arlington House Hunt

Directions: As you tour the house, look for each detail below.

1. In the center hall, find the ceiling lantern that is a copy of the one that G.W.P. Custis brought from Mount Vernon. How is this lantern lit? __________________________

2. In the family parlor, find the portrait of Mary Custis that was painted just before her marriage. Where is it located? ___________________

3. In the family dining room, look for the portrait of G.W.P. Custis over the fireplace. Also in the room are silhouettes. Where are they?

   ____

Climb the stairs and immediately turn to your right.

4. Can you find the small cupboard in the girls' dressing room? What is inside it? ____

5. How many girls shared the Lee girls' chamber? How did they climb into bed? ____

6. Mrs. Lee had two dressing rooms made into this small guest room. What craft is displayed? ______________________

7. Can you find a board game in the Lee boys' room that originally belonged to General Lee? What game is it? ______________

8. In the Lee's bedroom, find the chairs that can be made into writing desks. How does this happen? ______________

9. Look for the two white marble mantles in the White Parlor. What decorative pattern is carved into the marble? ______________

When you enter the morning room look for the huge painting of the Battle of Monmouth, painted by G.W.P. Custis. He painted many paintings in this room, most of them on Revolutionary War themes.

10. Look for the curved (convex) mirror hanging high on the wall. Why was it curved and hung so high up? ______________

Back to the Future

Can you find the raised tombstone in front of Arlington House? It is the gravesite of Pierre L' Enfant, the French engineer who designed the city of Washington. With all his grand plans, L' Enfant was difficult to work with and his plans were put aside. He died in 1825 a pauper and was buried on a friend's estate in Maryland. In the late 19th and early 20th centuries, however, the City Planning Commission revived L' Enfant's ideas. His body was moved to Arlington National Cemetery in 1909 to honor his contribution to our nation's Capital.

Mount Vernon

George Washington's Home

Getting Started . . .

Mount Vernon is the home of George Washington, our first President. He lived on this large farm, called a planation, for most of his life, except for the times he served his country as a military officer and as President. Although he spent a lot of time away from Mount Vernon, Washington always thought of himself as a farmer and eagerly looked forward to his return to the family farm. In 1799 President Washington died at Mount Vernon and is buried there.

Besides the large house, there are many small buildings on the grounds. The real work of the plantation took place in these out buildings. Cooking was done in the kitchen and spinning in the spinning cottage. In other buildings people did laundry, cleaned, and cared for the horses and carriages.

If you stand on the piazza (the big porch) and look across the Potomac River, you are looking at the same view that the Washingtons saw when they lived here more than 200 years ago. Many people want this

unspoiled view preserved so that future visitors to Mount Vernon will also be able to see it. At this time the National Park Service owns the land across the river.

When you tour the house you will discover things that were given to George and Martha Washington and other things that were purchased by the family. Other artifacts were made during the time that the family lived, although they might not have belonged to the President's family.

If you are visiting a lot of sights in this area, you will learn a great deal about the Civil War. Although there was fighting in northern Virginia, Mount Vernon was declared neutral ground. Many soldiers from both the North and the South visited George Washington's home, but they left their weapons at the gate.

Washington House Tour

Discover each item below while touring Mount Vernon. Check each item when you find it. Then answer the question that follows by filling in the blank.

1. When you start the tour you will be looking at the back of the house. Look carefully at the house. Is it made of brick or wood?
   ____

2. In the large dining room, can you find the symbols on the plaster ceiling? These symbols reminded Washington of his farm. Why?
   ____

3. When you step out on the large porch, called a piazza, what river do you see? ______________________

4. In the central passageway (the big hall with the staircase), find the key to La Bastille, the French prison. Who gave this key to George Washington? ______________________

Bedrooms:

5. Can you find the bedroom with Martha Washington's traveling trunk? When did she use it? ______________________

6. Can you find a crib that was given to Nelly Custis, Martha Washington's granddaughter, for her child? Who used the crib?
   ____

The Study:

8. In President Washington's study, find the special chair that was used to keep the flies away. It had a fan that moved back and forth. What made the fan move?______________________________

The Kitchen:

9. Visit the kitchen. Why was the kitchen separated from the rest of the house?___________________________________

Super History Sleuth

Call yourself a Super History Sleuth if you can find out something about Miss Sarah Tracy while you are touring. Hint: She had something to do with Mount Vernon during the Civil War.

Mount Vernon Cipher

Solve this picket fence cipher. Write the message on the blanks below.

Example: L O C R F L Y
O K A E U L = <u>LOOKCAREFULLY</u>

I B D E T E G O G
N A W A H R E R E

A H N T N S D O A E
W S I G O U E T T K

H S X R I E N H P A Z
I E E C S O T E I Z A

____

____

____

Answers

Can You Name These Buildings? Page 6

1. United States Capitol
2. National Gallery of Art
3. Museum of Natural History
4 The Washington Monument
5. Mount Vernon
6. The Jefferson Memorial

Capitol Art—Page 12

	Date	Artist
1.	1492	John Vanderlyn
2.	1541	William H. Powell
3.	1613	John G. Chapman
4.	1620	Robert W. Weir
5.	1776	John Trumbull
6.	1777	John Trumbul
7.	1781	John Trumbull
8.	1783	John Trumbull

Capitol Search—Page 13

1. detail of Freedom
2. Corncob column
3. tobacco leaves column
4. Car of History
5. Women's Suffrage Monument

Capitol Trivia—Page 13

Pocahontas appears in the frieze, a painting, and in a relief over the west door.

Supreme Court Trivia—Page 15

1. William Howard Taft
2. Sandra Day O'Connor
3. Byron White; his football name was Whizzer, because he could pass the football so well.
4. William O. Douglass
5. Oliver Wendell Holmes
6. John Jay

Judicial Maze—Page15

The correct route spells "Equal Justice Under Law."

Library of Congress Word Hunt Page 17

K N L N B X M M A H M E N R P U
I G P E R I O D I C A L A N A R
V Z E Q P H O T O S E O G W P M
G Z N A I O D Z N V F U V W E D
I C E E L O L X S A W I D I R D
L N N B G M U S I C C G L T S T
J J S Q G L B R T B X A E M N X
H R V T M S H R S V Q L I H S J
T V M W R J E F F E R S O N Y I
R O L Q E U J E H Q O C G S O R
M B I C Z C M V M A P S K V X I
N O B I I X H E A O X I T Q S F
Z O R Q Q Q H N N T Y B B Q W H
W K A X R W S N Q T S K I Z M F
E S R W R V H B U E S M N Z M J
A A Y C O P Y R I G H T L E Q Y
A J R U A X N Z D W O F M N R O

Interesting Names—Page 21

Starfighter: First fighter plane in the world to go twice the speed of sound, or Mach 2.
Voyager: In 1986 this unusual-looking plane made the first non-stop trip around the world in 9 days, 3 minutes, and 44 seconds.
GOES: Geostationary Operational Environmental Satellite. Moving at the same speed the earth rotates, it appears to stay in place as it monitors one region of the earth.
Winnie Mae: A plane owned by Wiley Post. Completed two world record flights in 1931 and 1933.
Grumman Goose: A plane designed for very wealthy Americans. The price was raised from $60,000 to $66,000 so that only the wealthiest people could afford it.
Glamorous Glynnis: Plane used by Air Force Captain Charles Yeager when he flew faster than the speed of sound on October 14, 1947.
Vin Fiz: A plane flown by Calbraith Perry Rogers on a world record flight across the country—4321 miles.

Rocket Word Hunt—Page 22

Flight Trivia—Page 22

All of these women were early pilots.

Fabulous Flying Feats Page 23

Amelia Earhart
First woman to make a solo airplane flight across the Atlantic Ocean.
Neil A. Armstrong
First man to walk on the moon on—July 20, 1969. "That's one small step for a man; one giant leap for mankind."
Engene Bullard and Bessie Coleman
First black Americans to become licensed pilots.
Charles Lindberg
Flew the first non-stop solo flight across the Atlantic.
Wilbur and Orville Wright
Flew the first power-driven airplane at Kitty Hawk in 1903.
Jacqueline Cochran
First woman to fly faster than the speed of sound.

Answers

Calder mobiles—Page 25
We found four:
"Stainless Stealer," above the escalator; "Zarabanda," and "Fish Mobile," level 3 balcony gallery; and "Two Disks," a mobile-stabile in the Sculpture Garden.

Three Sculptures—Page 25
1. Theseus Slaying the Centaur Bianor by Antoine-Louis Barye Bronze, 1850
2. Fish Mobile by Alexander Calder, 1940
3. Woman with Baby Carriage by Pablo Picasso Bronze after found objects, 1950. He used a piece of stovepipe, muffin tins, gear wheels, and other scraps.

Name Game—Page 27

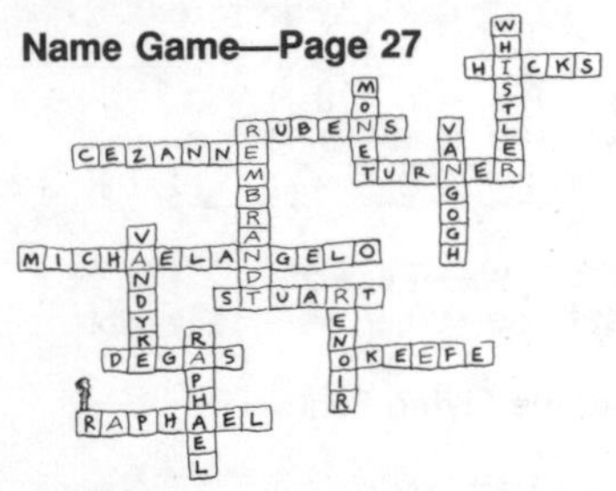

Pallet Puzzle—Page 28
1. Museum
2. Mobile
3. Brushes
4. Palette
5. Sculpture
6. Artist
7. Frames
8. Easel
9. Paintings

Great Word Hunt—Page 30

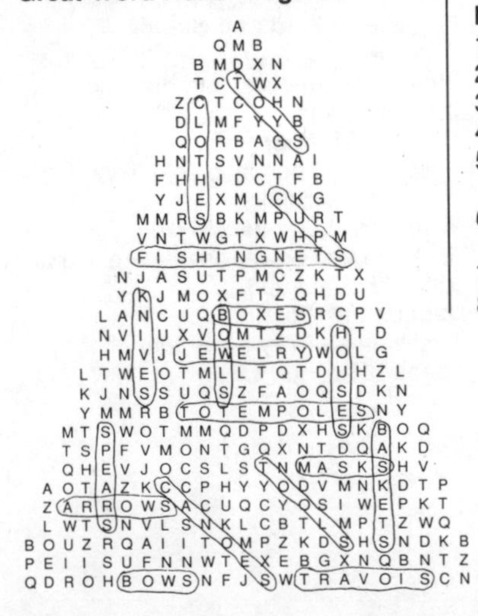

What Kind of Hunter Are You? Page 31

toys	wood, bone, ivory, cornhusks
houses	wood, grasses, skin, mats
masks	wood, husks, fur, hair, feathers
kayaks/ canoes	birchbark, bone, wood
knives	bone, wood, metal
jewelry	beads, shells, silver, animal sinew for stringing
spears	wood rods, metal stone
bowls	wood, clay
totem pole	wood, natural dyes from bark and plants

Crack This Code—Page 32
Arthropods come from a Latin word meaning jointed legs.

Insect Zoo Crossword Puzzle Page 33
Across:
2. Bee
5. Crab
6. Millipede
7. Tarantula
8. Grasshopper
10. Horseshoe Crab
11. Silkworm

Down:
1. Walking Stick
2. Butterfly
3. Mosquito
4. Praying Mantis
9. Cricket

Fossll Find—Page 34
1. Diplodocus
2. Triceratops
3. May have been an adult.
4. 40 feet long and 16 feet high
5. Tyrannasaurus, Diplophsaurus, Ceratosaurus, Deinorychus
6. Triceratops, Duckbills, Stegosau rus
7. Chisels, brushes, picks, rulers
8. Plaster

Artifact Search—Page 38
1. Iron toaster
2. Hackle and cover
3. Ceramic jug
4. Bell
5. Playing cards
6. First U.S. Treasury key
7. Surgeon's amputation saw
8. Wheelwright's traveler
9. Shoe sizing stick

Name Your Sport—Page39
We found football, tennis, ice skating, baseball, roller skating, lacrosse, racquetball, skiing, auto racing, cycling, boxing, golf, fishing, and soccer equipment.

Are You a Stamp Collector? Page 40
1. stone tablets
2. papyrus
3. horses
4. 100 BC

Postage Trivia—Page 40
Benjamin Franklin

View From The Top—Page 43
West: Lincoln Memorial and Reflecting Pool
North: The White House
East: The Capitol, The Mall, Smithsonian Buildings
South: The Jefferson Memorial, and the Tidal Basin

Can you find the answers to these questions?—Page 43
1. The Washington Monument cost $1,187,710
2. The monument sways slightly. In a 30 mph wind it will sway 0.125 of an inch.
3. The original design called for a circular, temple-like building with a giant statue of Washington and space for statues of other Presidents and national heroes.
4. 50 flags fly at the Washington Monument representing the number of states in the nation

Monumental Trivia—Page 43
The original plans called for a statue of George Washington on his horse.

Mural Match
Page 45
1. Four score and seven years ago our fathers brought forth on this continent a new nation/An Angel of Truth frees a slave
(Gettysburg Address)
2. Fellow Countrymen: At this second appearing to take the oath of office there is less occasion for an extended address/An Angel of Truth unites the hands of the North and the South.
(Second Inaugural Address)

Lincoln Memorial Scramble
Page 45
1. sixteenth
2. marble
3. pool
4. states

Lincoln Trivia—Page 46
1. February 12, 1809
2. Kentucky
3. read and write.
4. Indiana; Illinois.
5. six feet tall
6. Mary Todd.
8. Civil War.
9. Emancipation Proclaimation
10. John Wilkes Booth
11. train

Monumental Trivia—Page 46
Ionic ouside; Doric inside

Fill in the Missing Words
Page 48
1. . . . truth, created equal, that they are endowed by their Creator with certain unalienable rights, among these are life, liberty, and the pursuit of happiness.
—*The Declaration of Independence*
2. . . . laws and institutions must go hand in hand with the progress of the human mind. As that becomes more developed, more enlightened, as new discoveries are made, new truths discovered and manners and opinions change, with the change of circumstances, institutions must advance also to keep pace with the times.
3. I have sworn upon the alter of God eternal hostility against every form of tyranny over the mind of man.

Jefferson Trivia:—Page 48
The men portrayed above the main entry are Benjamin Franklin, John Adams, Roger Sherman and Robert R. Livingston, the men on the Continental Congress committee to write the *Declaration of Independence.*

Kennedy Center Search
Page 50
1. Great Britain—"Figure"
2. Egypt—Alabaster vase
3. Sweden—Orrefors chandeliers
4. "Poseidon"—Greece

Kennedy Center Crossword Puzzle
Page 51
Down
1. Concert Hall
2. marble
3. countries
4. three
5. Foyer
6. Potomac River

Across
5. flags
7. Kennedy
8. art
9. Eisenhower
10. Opera House

Explosive Art—Page 51
Apollo X 1970 was created by exploding dynamite on each side of steel that was then polished.

City Vista—Page 55
Left to right: Kennedy Center, Lincoln Memorial, Washington Monument, U.S. Capitol, Jefferson Memorial

Presidential Challenge
Page 56
"And so my fellow Americans: ask not what your country can do for you—ask what you can do for your country. My fellow citizens of the world: ask not what America will do for you, but what together we can do for the freedom of man."

Arlington House Hunt
Page 56-57
1. candles
2. over the mantle
3. on the wall
4. teaset
5. 4, steps
6. lacemaking
7. chess
8. the arms flip over
9. oak leaves
10. to reflect light into room

Washington House Tour
Page 59-60
1. wood
2. farm tools
3. Potomac River
4. General Lafayette
5. When she travelled to and from winter army quarters during the Revolution.
6. Nelly's baby
7. foot pedals
8. because of the danger of fire

Super History Sleuth—Page 60
Sarah Tracy live at Mount Vernon during the Civil War.

Mount Vernon Cipher
Page 60
In bad weather George Washington used to take his exercise on the piazza.

Mementos